STUMPTOWN™

PORTLAND, OREGON

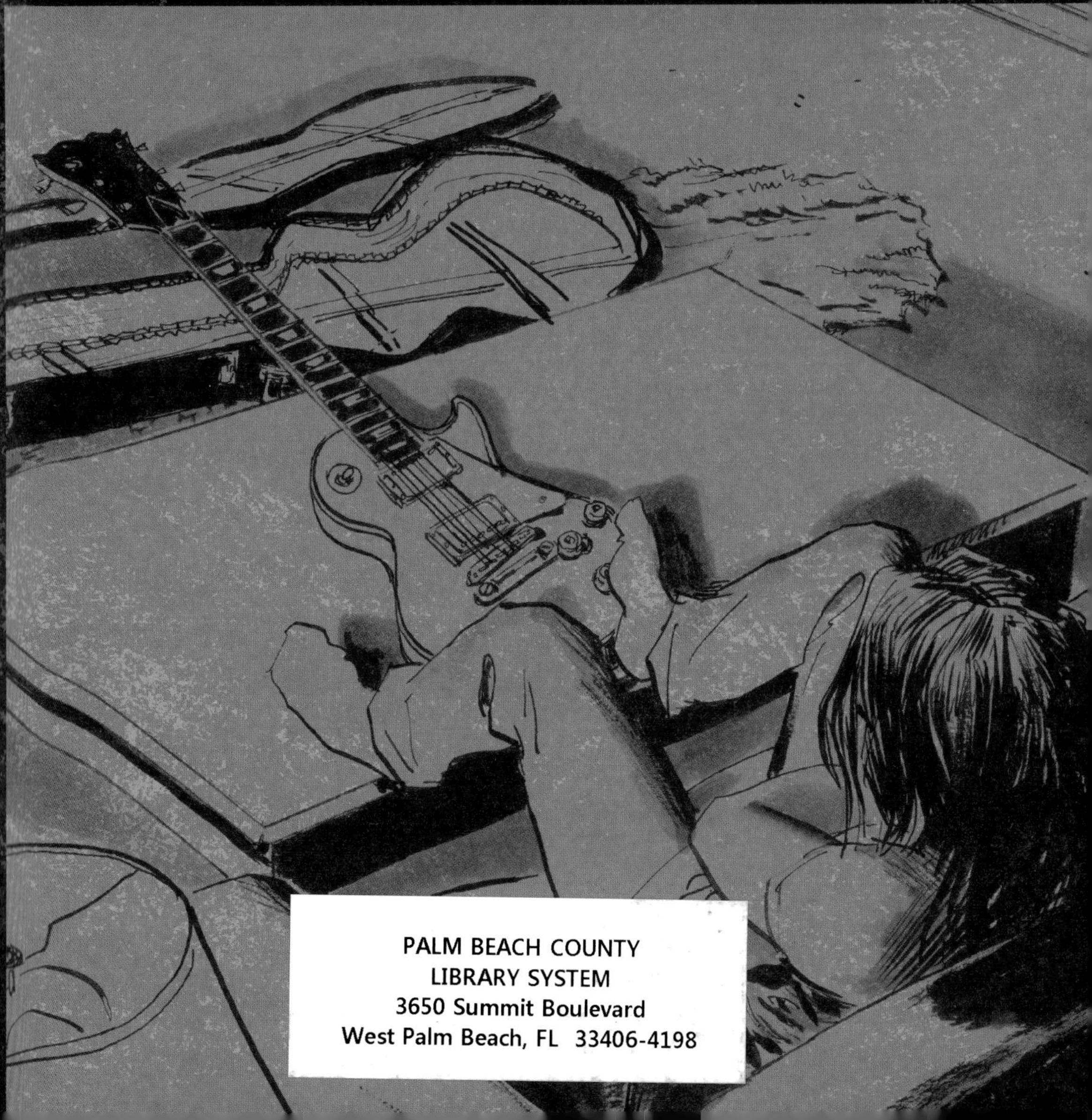

STUMPTOWN™

INVESTIGATIONS • PORTLAND, OREGON

The Case of the Baby in the Velvet Case

written by
GREG RUCKA

illustrated by
MATTHEW SOUTHWORTH

colored by
RICO RENZI with
MATTHEW SOUTHWORTH

Edited by
JAMES LUCAS JONES

Designed by
KEITH WOOD

AN ONI PRESS PRODUCTION

PUBLISHED BY ONI PRESS, INC.
Joe Nozemack, founder & chief financial officer
James Lucas Jones, publisher
Charlie Chu, v.p. of creative & business development Brad
Rooks, director of operations
Rachel Reed, marketing manager
Melissa Meszaros, publicity manager
Troy Look, director of design & production
Hilary Thompson, senior graphic designer
Kate Z. Stone, junior graphic designer
Angie Dobson, digital prepress lead
Ari Yarwood, executive editor
Robin Herrera, senior editor
Desiree Wilson, associate editor
Alissa Sallah, administrative assistant
Jung Lee, logistics associate

ONI PRESS, INC.
1319 SE Martin Luther King, Jr. Blvd.
Suite 240
Portland, OR 97214

onipress.com
facebook.com/onipress
twitter.com/onipress
onipress.tumblr.com
instagram.com/onipress
onipress.com

@ruckawriter / gregrucka.com
@mattsouthworth / matthewsouthworth.net
@whoisrico / nolongermint.com

First Edition: April 2018
978-1-62010-480-4

1 3 5 7 9 10 8 6 4 2

Library of Congress Control Number: 2017913119

Printed in China.

Chapter One

TAILHOOK
ZEE DEE OH
WE PA
CAS
TAILHOO
ZEE DEE OH
HERMAN and the HERETICS
OCTOBER 8
BALLROOM
2 BR / 1 BA
LOS
(206) 3

the last time that was the last time
I let you have me
I let you hold me

DANCE

CRYSTAL
TONIGHT
TAILHOOK
W ZEE DEE OHHH
AND HERMAN AND
THE HERETICS
BALLROOM

that was the last time the last time
I let you
burn me
burn me
burn me

the
last
time

tits

I let you
hold
meeee

I let you hold
meeee down

VANESSA! OUTSTAND--
BITE ME, GRAHAM.
EXIT
VAN, HOLD ON!
DAMMIT, HOLD ON!
BITE.
ME.

ANY IDEA WHAT THAT'S ABOUT?
DOES SHE NEED A REASON?
PUT IT LIKE THAT, NO.
YOU GOING TO THE AFTER PARTY?
I WAS THINKING OF GOING HOME...
...YOU KNOW, SLEEP IN MY OWN BED FOR THE FIRST TIME IN SIX MONTHS.
THANKS, FABRIZIO.
ALONE?
RED '79 LE
ALONE, ALAS.
EASY ENOUGH TO FIX THAT, MIM. JUST LEAN OUT THE STAGE DOOR.
YOU BEEN TAKING LESSONS FROM VAN, CLICK?
FUCK NO...
...I DON'T HAVE THE SEXUAL STAMINA...

BANG
BANG
BANG
BANG

PARK
PAY
TO PARK
ALL HOURS
24 HOURS

BANG
BANG
BANG
BANG
BANGUNK

OW!

GO BY UNION TRAIN STATION
OWMOTHERFU--
MMFFM
SORRY?
EXCUSE ME?
STUMPTOWN INVESTIGATIONS?
--DEX PARIOS, OWNER, PROPRIETOR, PRIMARY INVESTIGATOR. NICE TO MEET YOU.
HARRISON, DON HARRISON.
SO, WHAT CAN I DO FOR YOU, MISTER HARRISON?
I NEED, AH... I'M FOREMAN ON A SITE UP IN SULLIVAN'S GULCH. PUTTING UP THE NEW CONDOS THERE.
THING IS, I, I MEAN, WE'VE BEEN, THERE'RE... SEE, SUPPLIES, THEY'RE GOING MISSING, AND I DON'T, I MEAN, I NEED... AH...

YOU NEED SOMEONE TO COME IN AND PUT A STOP TO IT. MAYBE FIND OUT WHO'S DOING IT.
YES. YES, THAT'S IT, THAT'S IT EXACTLY. EXACTLY.
YOU'VE REPORTED THE THEFTS TO THE POLICE?
I HAVE, BUT IT'S, IT'S LOW PRIORITY, RIGHT NOW, I THINK.
I'M NOT LOOKING FOR *RECOVERY,* JUST... I NEED IT TO *STOP,* YOU SEE?
SURE. WELL, I CAN HELP YOU WITH THAT, SET UP SURVEILLANCE ON THE SITE, EVEN COME ON AS PART OF THE *CREW,* IF YOU'D RATHER.
FOR THIS I'D TAKE FIVE HUNDRED AS A RETAINER, SAY THIRTY BUCKS AN HOUR AGAINST THAT. YOU COVER EXPENSES.
THAT'LL BE FINE.
I'LL JUST PUT YOU DOWN AS THE *CLIENT,* THEN? DONALD HARRISON?
NO, THE COMPANY SHOULD BE THE CLIENT...
...RAIN OR SHINE CONSTRUCTION...

...I'M WRITING THE CHECK ON THE BUSINESS ACCOUNT--
YEAH.
DON'T BOTHER.
I-- WHAT?
I CAN'T TAKE THE JOB.
I'M SORRY TO HAVE WASTED YOUR TIME, MISTER HARRISON.
IF YOU'D LIKE, I CAN RECOMMEND ONE OR TWO OTHER FIRMS IN TOWN THAT'D BE HAPPY TO HELP YOU.
MALCOLM CLARK AT VIGILANT IS A GOOD GUY, YOU CAN TELL HIM I SENT YOU.
IF THIS IS A MONEY THING, I MEAN, I'VE GOT ROOM TO NEGOTIATE.
IT'S NOT A MONEY THING. BELIEVE ME, I COULD USE THE JOB.
RAIN OR SHINE IS A HECTOR MARENCO BUSINESS.
I DON'T DO WORK FOR HECTOR MARENCO.

"WHAT IS IN THAT WORD, HONOR; WHAT IS THAT HONOR?"
"AIR."
"A TRIM RECKONING? WHO HATH IT?"
"HE THAT DIED O'WEDNESDAY."

HENRY THE FOURTH, PART ONE, RIGHT?
AH... YEAH.
FALSTAFF, END OF ACT FIVE, SCENE ONE.
SO... YOU JUST NORMALLY STAND AROUND YOUR OFFICE, QUOTING SHAKESPEARE?
ASSUMING THIS IS YOUR OFFICE?
IT'S MY OFFICE. YOU STICK AROUND, I'LL DO THE MERRY WIVES OF WINDSOR NEXT.
YOU'RE MIRIAM BRACCA. TAILHOOK.
WOW, YOU REALLY ARE A DETECTIVE. MOST PEOPLE DON'T RECOGNIZE ME.
MOSTLY, THEY RECOGNIZE VAN.
I CHEATED. TRACY HOFFMAN'S A FRIEND OF MINE.
WHAT CAN I DO FOR YOU, MISS BRACCA?
SOMEONE STOLE MY BABY.

"I OWN... I OWN A FUCKTON OF GUITARS, UNDERSTAND ME. I THINK ALL OF US DO, ALL OF US WHO PLAY THEM, I MEAN. IT'S LIKE... NOT FETISH, NOT *COLLECTING,* BUT...
Rolling Stone
The Fraud at the Heart of the Mortgage Meltdown
EMINEM The Road Back From Hell
TAILHOOK The Making of a Masterpiece
"...THEY'RE *ART,* AND THEY'RE THE ART BY WHICH WE MAKE *ART,* IF THAT MAKES SENSE? CAPITAL 'A' *ART.*
NOVEMBER 2008
"I'VE GOT A '52 FENDER BROADCASTER, ORIGINAL FITTINGS, ANOTHER FENDER TELE THE LABEL GAVE ME WHEN *BLACK TAROT* WENT PLATINUM. I'VE GOT... I'VE GOT A LOT OF GUITARS.
"BUT THIS ONE, THIS ONE'S MY *BABY,* YOU UNDERSTAND? THIS IS MY *TRUE LOVE.*

"ALWAYS FAITHFUL, ALWAYS STEADY, ALWAYS THERE FOR ME. ALWAYS ALIVE UNDER MY FINGERS, ALWAYS READY TO SING. SO FULL OF SONGS, I CAN'T--I CAN'T **EXPLAIN** IT, IT'S JUST...THERE ARE SO MANY **SONGS** STILL IN HER.
"SHE'S A 1977 GIBSON LES PAUL, AND SHE'S **PERFECT.** ORIGINAL FITTINGS, FINGERBOARD TO THE PAF HUMBUCKERS, EVEN THE TAILPIECE AND THE BRIDGE.
"ONLY THING I DID TO IT WAS SHAVE AND SAND THE BACK OF THE NECK, JUST SO MY HAND WOULDN'T STICK TO THE LACQUER WHEN I PLAYED.
TREBLE
"SHE'S BEAUTIFUL.
"AND NOW SHE'S **GONE.**"

NOT TO BE CRUDE, BUT HOW MUCH IS "BABY" WORTH?

OH, WELL, SOME OF THEM, THEY SELL FOR HUNDREDS OF THOUSANDS OF DOLLARS. BUT *MINE?*

MY FOSTER DAD BOUGHT IT FOR ME WHEN I GRADUATED HIGH SCHOOL, IT WAS A PAWNSHOP GUITAR. HE PAID MAYBE $750 FOR IT, TOPS.

AND BECAUSE IT'S *YOURS?*

OH.

UHM... I DON'T KNOW. MAYBE MORE THAN THAT?

NIGHT BEFORE LAST. WE CLOSED OUT THE LATEST TOUR AT THE CRYSTAL BALLROOM.
FIFTY CITIES, ENDED UP BACK HOME.
WHAT HAPPENS TO YOUR GUITARS AFTER A SHOW?

THE ROADIES DO THE TAKEDOWN, JASON TAKES CARE OF CLICK'S KIT, FABRIZIO HANDLES MY GUITARS.
FABRIZIO?
FABRIZIO PULLANO, MY ***GUITAR TECH.***

HE TAKES EACH GUITAR, WIPES THEM DOWN, RESTRINGS THEM, WORKS THE HARDWARE, TUNES THEM. LIKE THAT.
YOU DON'T DO THAT YOURSELF?
I CAN, BUT... FABRIZIO'S SO MUCH ***BETTER*** AT IT THAN I AM. I PLAY BETTER BECAUSE OF HIM.

AND THEN?

DEPENDS. ON THE ROAD, THEY GET PACKED AND SHIPPED WITH THE REST OF THE GEAR TO THE NEXT GIG.
BUT I'M HOME, SO ALL MY GUITARS GOT DELIVERED TO MY HOUSE YESTERDAY AFTERNOON. EXCEPT BABY.

AND YOU ALREADY TALKED TO FABRIZIO?
RIGHT AWAY. HE WAS *REALLY* UPSET.
HE TOLD ME HE'D PACKED IT UP WITH THE REST OF THE GUITARS.

YOU SOUND *SURPRISED.*

DO I? I DON'T *MEAN* TO.
FABRIZIO LOVES THOSE GUITARS EVEN MORE THAN *I* DO, MS. PARIOS. AND BEFORE YOU THINK THAT MAKES HIM A *SUSPECT,* IT *DOESN'T.*
IT MAKES HIM A *BRILLIANT* GUITAR TECH.
DEX.

CALL ME DEX.
MIM.

THAT'S PROBABLY ENOUGH TO GET *STARTED.*
IT IS? DON'T YOU WANT TO TALK TERMS? A CONTRACT?

FIVE HUNDRED DOLLARS RETAINER, WE'LL WORK AN HOURLY RATE.
I'LL TALK TO MR. PULLANO, TAKE IT FROM THERE.

IF YOU SAY SO.
I *DO* HAVE ONE *MORE* QUESTION FOR YOU, THOUGH.
HMM?

ANY REASON YOU DIDN'T GO TO TRACY WITH THIS?
TRACY'S *POLICE*.
I'M IN A *ROCK 'N' ROLL* BAND.
YOU DO THE *MATH*.

WILL A THOUSAND BE ENOUGH TO COVER THINGS FOR NOW?
MORE THAN ENOUGH. I THOUGHT YOU AND SHE WERE--
NOT *ANYMORE*.

JUST... LOOK, *FORGET* ABOUT DETECTIVE HOFFMAN.
I DON'T WANT HER INVOLVED IN THIS, I DON'T WANT *ANYTHING* FROM HER AT ALL.

JUST FIND ME MY *BABY*.

UNION STATION
GO BY TRAIN
THERE SHE IS...
WHO'S THAT WITH HER?
NO IDEA, BUT IT MAKES A GOOD PHOTO.
WHICH DO YOU WANT?
I'LL TAKE THE NEW GIRL...
...YOU STICK WITH THE ROCK STAR.
KEEP IN TOUCH.
YEAH.
YOU TOO.
Nikon

--SAID *WHERE IS* IT?
STOP IT!! *LEAVE* HIM *ALONE!!*
SHUT THAT *BITCH* UP!
GED YUR *HANDS* UFF--
HE'S GONNA DO *MORE* THAN JUST *HOLD* HER, YOU DON'T START *TALKING,* YOU FUCKING *DAGO!*

WHERE IS IT? WHERE'S THE GUITAR?!?
I DUN KNOW! I DUN KNOW!!!
WRONG ANSWER--
THREE MINUTES.
ONE HUNDRED AND EIGHTY SECONDS.
WELL, ONE HUNDRED AND FIFTY, NOW, PROBABLY.
BITCH, YOU WALKED INTO THE WRONG HOUSE.
ONE FORTY, MAYBE.

THE FUCK IS SHE *TALKING* ABOUT, BRAD?
GOD *DAMMIT*--

--DON'T *USE* MY FUCKING *NAME!*
TWO MINUTES.

SHUT THE *FUCK* UP!
SHUT THE FUCK *UP* OR I CUT YOU A *NEW* SLIT, BITCH!
ONE-TEN.

...WHICH MEANS YOU'VE GOT ABOUT HALF THAT TIME LEFT TO VANISH.
Stop Watch
00:01:29.6
Lap
Stop
SAMSUNG
BRAD! WE GOTTA--
SHUT UP!
YOU...YOU'RE FULL OF SHIT.
TAKE THE TIME TO STAB ME AND YOU'LL FIND OUT.
BRAAAAD--
GET TO THE TRUCK--

--DEAL WITH *THEM* LATER...

...'SPECIALLY *YOU*, BITCH.

UH-OH! HEAR *THAT?*

THAT SOUNDS LIKE *SIRENS!*

FABRIZIO PULLANO? I'M DEX PARIOS.
YOU TWO OKAY? ASIDE FROM THE BLOODY NOSE?
WE ARE NOT OKAY!
PEOPLE BARGING INTO OUR HOME, ATTACKING US!
AND YOU, MISS, YOU-- I WOULD THANK YOU TO LEAVE, RIGHT NOW!
SURE, I'LL DO THAT. I JUST HAD A QUESTION OR TWO.
THOSE GUYS, THEY WERE LOOKING FOR THE BABY?
THE BABY? WHAT BABY?
DE GUIDAR. MIM CALLZ ID HUR 'BAYBEE'.
DEY BROKE MA NODE.
YEAH, MIM HIRED ME TO FIND IT.
AND I THINK THEY DID. MRS. PULLANO? YOU MIGHT WANT TO GET SOME ICE FOR YOUR HUSBAND--
HANDS.
OH FOR THE LOVE OF--

the case of the baby in the velvet case

Chapter Two

SOUTHWORTH
Supro

the case of the baby in the velvet case

part two

I'M TALKING TO MISTER PULLANO, HERE.
SO THESE GUYS, THESE TWO GUYS--
SKINHEADS.
--THEY JUST *BROKE* IN, THEY GRABBED YOU, YOUR WIFE.
YOU'D NEVER SEEN THEM BEFORE, NEVER EVEN MET THEM BEFORE?
NEBBER DEEN DEM 'AFOR.
YOU WANT THE ONE WITH THE BROKEN NOSE.
DID YOU GET *NAMES* OFF THEM, ANYTHING?
NO IDEA WHO THESE GUYS WERE AT *ALL?*
THEY WERE SKINHEADS.
ONE CALLED MICK, THE OTHER--THE TALLER--WAS NAMED BRAD.

OUTSIDE.
WHAT, ALONE?
*OUT*SIDE.
YOU A *HARD* CASE, PARIOS?
OOOH, AGENT CHASE KNOWS MY *NAME.*
WAIT...
...YOU WERE FOLLOWING ME? RAN MY *LICENSE PLATE,* MAYBE?
WHY FOLLOW ME?
YOU WERE FOLLOWING BRACCA *FIRST.* THAT'S IT, ISN'T IT?
THAT HAS TO BE IT.

THAT'S *INTERESTING.* THAT'S KINDA... THAT'S *FASCINATING.*
WHY IS THE *D.E.A.* FOLLOWING MY *CLIENT?*
I ASKED YOU A *QUESTION.*
YEAH, BUT I JUST ASKED YOU A *BETTER* ONE.
GO AWAY NOW.
WHY'S THE D.E.A. FOLLOWING MY CLIENT?
GO. AWAY.
NOW.
THIS ABOUT THE *GUITAR?*

YOU'RE KIDDING ME.
THIS *IS* ABOUT THE ***GUITAR?***
SHUT. UP. AND.
LISTEN.

YOU'VE WANDERED INTO A ***FEDERAL*** INVESTIGATION.
YOU'VE GOT ***NO RIGHT*** TO BE HERE.

STAY ***OUT*** OF IT. STAY ***CLEAR*** OF IT. GO DO YOUR ***LAUNDRY*** OR SOMETHING AND THEN BILL THE ***ROCK STAR*** YOUR HOURLY RATE.
BUT STAY THE ***HELL*** OUT OF THIS.

GO BY TRAIN
UNION STATION
2009 FILES
HEY, YOU'VE REACHED MIM. YOU KNOW THE SONG.
DEET
MISS BRACCA, IT'S DEX PARIOS.
I NEED YOU TO CALL ME AS SOON AS YOU GET THIS, PLEASE.
BIP
BEG PARDON...
...ARE YOU DEXEDRINE PARIOS?
DEX.
I BEG YOU, PLEASE, CALL ME DEX.

I'M DAVID MAYES.
I'M IN TAILHOOK WITH MIM BRACCA.
CLICK. RIGHT!
STAGE NAME, JUST... YOU KNOW, DAVID.
DAVID, SURE. NICE TO MEET YOU, DAVID.
TAKE A, AH... WELL, IF YOU CAN FIND A SEAT, AT LEAST...
STANDING'S FINE, THANKS.
HOW CAN I HELP YOU?
I TALKED TO MIM. SHE SAYS YOU'RE LOOKING FOR HER BABY FOR HER.
DID SHE?

HEH.
YEAH, DISCRETION IS GOOD, I APPRECIATE THAT.
NOT A LOT OF DISCRETION IN TAILHOOK?

DEPENDS WHO YOU'RE TALKING ABOUT.
ME? I'M VERY DISCREET.

AND MIM?
SHE'S NEVER BEEN COMFORTABLE WITH ATTENTION. NO IDEA HOW TO DEAL WITH IT, EVEN NOW.
NOW, VAN... THAT GIRL WAS BORN FOR THE SPOTLIGHT.
THIS YOU?

YEAH, ABOUT FIVE YEARS AGO.

IRAQ OR AFGHANISTAN?
YES.
REGULAR ARMY OR RESERVES?

YOU DON'T WANT TO TALK ABOUT *MY* PAST, MISTER MAYES.
DAVID.
AND YOU'RE *SURE* OF THAT, ARE YOU?

LOOK, IF YOU'RE HERE TO ASK ABOUT MY INVESTIGATION, I CAN'T REALLY--
NAH, I KINDA WANTED TO TALK TO YOU ABOUT MIM, IS ALL.
YOU'RE WORRIED ABOUT HER?

WORRY ABOUT HER ALL THE TIME. VAN, SHE'S *HIGH*-MAINTENANCE. GRAHAM--OUR MANAGER--HE'S GOT BOTH HANDS FULL TRYING TO KEEP HER HAPPY.
ME, I'M EASY, YOU KNOW? PLAY MY DRUMS, DRINK MY BEER, MAYBE WASTE A DAY PLAYING VIDEO GAMES. *LOW* MAINTENANCE. BUT MIM...

...COUPLE YEARS AGO THINGS GOT *BAD* FOR HER. HER OLD MAN WAS ACCUSED OF *MURDERING* HER *BROTHER*, SHE WAS BEING *STALKED*, NAKED *PICTURES* POSTED ONLINE, ALL OF IT.
...I DON'T WANT TO SEE HER GO THROUGH ANYTHING LIKE THAT *AGAIN*.

AND YOU THINK THE *GUITAR* DISAPPEARING MIGHT BE THE START OF HISTORY *REPEATING* ITSELF?
THINK IT? NO.
FEAR IT? HELL, YEAH.

IT COULD BE NOTHING, YOU KNOW? FANS DO WEIRD SHIT. I MEAN, REALLY WEIRD SHIT.
OR IT COULD BE SOMEONE TRYING TO MAKE A BUCK. A LOT OF MUSICIANS GET THEIR INSTRUMENTS STOLEN...

...PUT UP ON E-BAY, SOLD TO PRIVATE COLLECTORS.
HELL, ONE OF THE DECEMBERISTS HAD AN ACCORDION STOLEN LAST YEAR AND HELD FOR RANSOM.

HAPPENS MORE THAN YOU'D THINK.
YOU THINK YOU COULD GET ME A LIST OF THE SUPPORT CREW FOR THIS LAST TOUR? NAMES AND NUMBERS, LIKE THAT?
ROADIES, YOU MEAN? SHOULD BE ABLE TO, YEAH.

YOU THINK ONE OF THEM TOOK THE BABY?
OR MAYBE SAW WHOEVER DID.
THIS IS THE NUMBER FOR MY CELL, AND MY EMAIL, TOO. IF YOU CAN SEND ME THE LIST...

...AS SOON AS YOU GET IT...

I'LL SEE WHAT I CAN DO FOR YOU.

THANKS FOR THE TIME.
NICE TO MEET YOU, DEX.
YEAH...
...YOU, TOO.
DA-DEE DA-DA-DA-DEE-DA

NOK NOK
NOK NOK

UHM...
...HI?
I TRIED THE FRONT DOOR.
CAN'T *HEAR* IT WHEN I'M DOWN HERE.
THIS IS... THIS IS YOUR *MUSIC* ROOM?
IT'S NICE.
REALLY NICE.
YEAH.
HOW ABOUT WE GO UPSTAIRS?

BUT... WHY WOULD THE *D.E.A.* BE FOLLOWING *ME?*

I WAS HOPING YOU COULD ANSWER THAT, ACTUALLY.
I DON'T EVEN *USE* DRUGS!

YOU'RE A ROCK STAR.
I *DON'T!*
I'M A *MUSICIAN.*
A MUSICIAN WHO PLAYS *SOLD-OUT* CONCERTS AROUND THE WORLD AND HAS MULTI-MILLION SELLING *ALBUMS.*

I'M AN ALCOHOLIC.

BEEN SOBER JUST OVER THREE AND A HALF YEARS, NOW.

I DON'T DRINK, I DON'T DO DRUGS.
SEX?
NOT NEARLY ENOUGH.
YOU SAID...
...WAS FABRIZIO ALL RIGHT? I SHOULD CALL HIM, I NEED TO CALL--
HE'S OKAY. BUSTED NOSE THAT'S ALL.
THAT'S ALL.
YOU TALK TO DAVID TODAY? TELL HIM YOU'D HIRED ME?
DAVID?
CLICK.
YEAH. WHY?
NO REASON.

WHEN YOU CAME TO ME, I ASKED WHY YOU HADN'T GONE TO TRACY ABOUT THE *GUITAR*.
YOU GAVE ME SOME LINE ABOUT BEING IN A BAND.
IT WASN'T SOME *LINE*.
WE STOPPED SEEING EACH OTHER, IT WASN'T *PRETTY*, OKAY?
FINE, BUT THERE ARE *OTHER* COPS ASIDE FROM YOUR *EX*.
AND YOU KEPT SAYING *NO COPS*.
MISSING GUITAR, D.E.A. INVESTIGATION, SKINHEADS BREAKING YOUR GUITAR TECH'S *NOSE*.
SOUNDS TO ME LIKE *SMUGGLING* SOMETHING, MIM. IF I HAD TO TAKE A GUESS, I'D SAY SMUGGLING *METH*.
AND YOU SAYING NO COPS, THAT MAKES YOU LOOK *INVOLVED*.
WAIT--WHAT? YOU THINK...
...*SMUGGLING?*
THINK ABOUT IT...

"...YOU'VE BEEN TOURING FOR WHAT, JUST UNDER A YEAR? ALL AROUND THE COUNTRY, ALL AROUND THE WORLD, MAYBE?
"...ALL THOSE CASES, ALL THOSE CONTAINERS, ALL THOSE CITIES.
"ALL THAT EQUIPMENT'S GOT TO COME WITH YOU...
PARAMOUNT
"EASY TO MAKE A CONNECTION IN ONE TOWN OR ANOTHER, MAYBE GIVE SOMEONE A BACKSTAGE PASS OR SOMETHING.
CREW
"MAKE THE DEAL BEFORE, DURING, OR AFTER THE SHOW...
"...JUST WAIT UNTIL THE BREAKDOWN IS FINISHED, WAIT FOR THE RIGHT MOMENT...
CREW
PARAMOUNT
PRESENTS
TAILHOOK
THE CAPILLARIES
JUNE 7 8 PM
PACKWOOD
"...TUCK IT INTO SOME CORNER OF SOME BOX, HIDE IT UNDER SOMETHING, AND THERE YOU GO."

IT'S NOT THE BEST METHOD, MAYBE, BUT IT WOULD WORK.
IT'S A THEORY, AT LEAST.
AND YOU PUT THAT NEXT TO NO COPS...
I DON'T WANT THE COPS INVOLVED BECAUSE I DON'T WANT ANYONE TO GET INTO TROUBLE!
SHIT HAPPENS, OKAY?!?
PEOPLE DRINK, PEOPLE DO DRUGS, PEOPLE FUCK!
BUT IT'S NOT-- IT'S NOT SMUGGLING, IT'S NOT, LIKE, ORGANIZED CRIME!
I'M JUST TRYING TO PROTECT THE BAND.
I JUST WANT TO PROTECT THE BAND.

I DON'T NEED THE D.E.A. CRAWLING UP MY ASS FOR A CLIENT WHO WON'T GIVE ME THE TRUTH, MIM.
IF THERE'S SOMEONE YOU'RE TRYING TO PROTECT, I NEED TO KNOW THAT.
IF THERE'S SOMETHING YOU'RE NOT TELLING ME, I NEED TO HEAR IT NOW.
I'M NOT, I SWEAR TO GOD.
I JUST WANT MY BABY BACK.
I'VE GOT TO GET HOME, CHECK ON MY BROTHER.
I'LL CALL YOU TOMORROW.

HEY! ANSEL! GREY! I'M *HOME!*
UP-UP *STAIRS,* DEX!
L-L-*LISTEN,* DEX!
GREY IS PLAYING YOUR NEW GUITAR!
MY--WAIT, WHAT?
DEX! HOPE YOU DON'T MIND...
...I'VE NEVER GOTTEN TO PLAY ONE LIKE *THIS* BEFORE.
WHEN'D YOU START PLAYING GUITAR?

Chapter Three

the case of the baby in the velvet case

part three

HOW DID IT GET HERE?
THERE WAS A *MAN* AT THE *DOOR.*
AT THE DOOR.
WHAT MAN?
DID HE GIVE A *NAME?*
HE SAID... HE SAID IT WAS F-FOR *YOU.*
IS THAT *ALL?*
ANSEL? DO YOU *REMEMBER* ANYTHING ELSE?

I D-D-DON'T REM-ME-REME-REMEMBER!

WHAT?
YOU DIDN'T HAVE TO BE MEAN.
I WASN'T BEING MEAN.

THEN THAT WAS A GREAT IMPRESSION OF IT.
SO I'M NOT SUPPOSED TO ASK? I'M NOT SUPPOSED TO FIND OUT WHERE THE HELL IT CAME FROM?
I KNOW MY BROTHER HAS DOWN'S, GREY, OKAY? I'M WELL AWARE OF HIS ABILITIES AND HIS LIMITS.
ANSEL DOESN'T NEED TO BE CODDLED.
WHY ARE YOU SO UPSET? THAT'S IT, RIGHT? THAT'S THE GUITAR?
MIM BRACCA'S GUITAR, MIM FROM TAILHOOK? HER GUITAR?
YES, IT'S HER GUITAR.
I TOTALLY WAS PLAYING MIM BRACCA'S GUITAR.

IT'S JUST... IT'S A REALLY NICE GUITAR, THE ACTION IS AMAZING, I BET IF YOU PLUGGED IT IN, THE TONE ON IT WOULD JUST...
MAYBE YOU'D LIKE TO BE ALONE WITH IT FOR A LITTLE WHILE?
WELL... CASE CLOSED, NOW, RIGHT?
YOU CAN CALL HER UP AND NOT TELL HER I PLAYED IT AND LET HER KNOW YOU'VE FOUND BABY.
YEAH.
NO.
YEAH NO? WHY YEAH NO?
THE D.E.A. IS LOOKING FOR THE GUITAR.
SO CALL THE D.E.A., THEN.
...OR NOT?
I'M LOOKING FOR BABY, BABY JUST HAPPENS TO SHOW UP ON MY FRONT FUCKING DOORSTEP?
THE GUITAR. THE GUITAR JUST SHOWS UP.
CHRIST, NOW I'M DOING IT, TOO.
Standard

MAYBE WHOEVER TOOK IT FELT GUILTY?
OKAY, CLEARLY I'M *TWO* FOR *TWO* HERE, SO I'LL JUST *SHUT UP* FOR NOW, HOW ABOUT *THAT*?
UNLESS YOU'RE GOING FOR THREE OUT OF THREE, THAT'S AN IDEA.
Gibson
Gibson

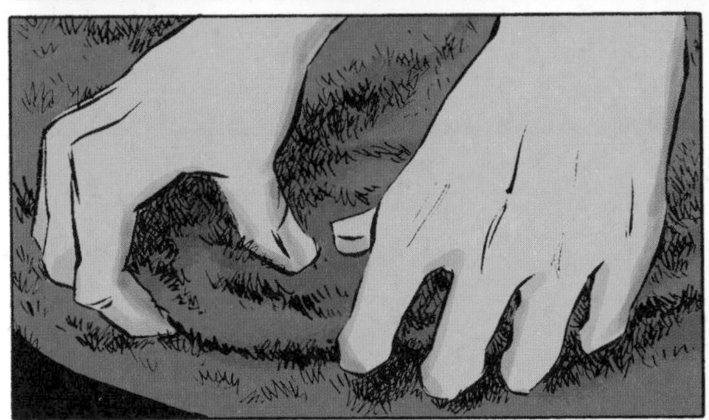

SHIT.
SHIT?
IF SOMETHING WAS BEING ***SMUGGLED,*** IT'S ***GONE.***

BUT THAT'S ***GOOD,*** RIGHT? MEANS SHE WASN'T INVOLVED?
ALL IT ***MEANS*** IS THAT THERE'S ***NOTHING*** IN THE CASE ***NOW,*** GREY.

DOESN'T MEAN THERE WASN'T SOMETHING IN THE CASE TO BEGIN WITH.
I'M BACK TO CASE CLOSED. CALL HER UP AND GIVE HER BABY BACK.
WHY?
...BECAUSE SHE'S YOUR CLIENT AND IT'S HER GUITAR?
NO, WHY RETURN THE GUITAR? WHY NOT JUST DUMP IT AFTER YOU'D EMPTIED THE CASE OR WHATEVER?
YOU KNOW HOW MUCH BABY IS WORTH, DEX? CLAPTON GUITARS GO FOR TWO MILLION DOLLARS AT AUCTION.
MIM'S NOT CLAPTON, BUT... THAT'S MAYBE A MILLION BUCKS THERE. MAYBE.
YOU JUST MADE MY POINT.
...SO I HAVE.
TALK TO YOU LATER, GREY.
THANKS FOR EVERYTHING.

ANSEL?
HEY. ANSEL.
I KNOW YOU CAN HEAR ME.
N-NO I *CAN'T.*
IT'S NOT *ON,* ANSEL.
MENU
I ST-STILL *CAN'T* HEAR Y-Y-YOU.
NU-UH.

I'M SORRY I WAS MEAN.
H-HE HAD GLASSES.
HE HAD GLASSES.
THANKS, ANSEL.

WHO'VE YOU BEEN OUT WITH, BABY?

WHERE'VE YOU BEEN?

Peet's Coffee

I DON'T LIKE YOU.

YOU *HAVE* TO HAVE FIGURED THAT MUCH OUT BY NOW.
I'M A *SLOW* LEARNER, AGENT CHASE.
DEX PARIOS...

...NICE TO MEET YOU.
MIKE VELA. PLEASURE.
YEAH, YEAH, YEAH, ALL VERY NICE...

...YOU WANTED TO MEET, WE'RE MEETING.
TALK.

LET ME SHOW YOU SOMETHING.

THINK YOU GUYS WERE LOOKING FOR THIS.

WHERE'D YOU GET IT?
SOMEONE DROPPED IT OFF AT MY HOUSE LAST NIGHT WHILE I WAS OUT.
ACCORDING TO MY BROTHER, SOMEONE WHO WEARS *GLASSES*.

WE'LL NEED TO TALK TO HIM.
NO.
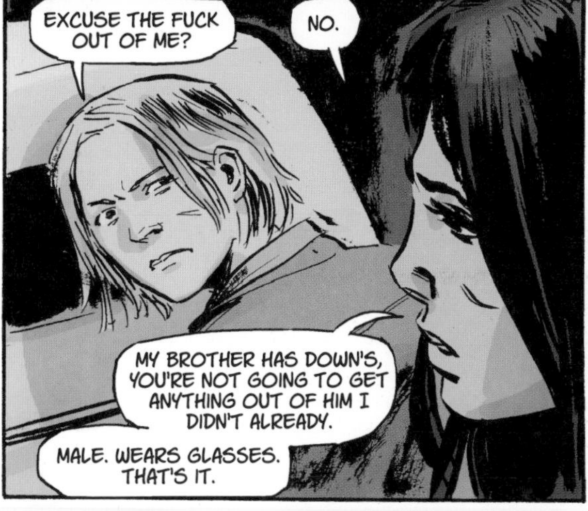
EXCUSE THE FUCK OUT OF ME?
NO.
MY BROTHER HAS DOWN'S, YOU'RE NOT GOING TO GET ANYTHING OUT OF HIM I DIDN'T ALREADY.
MALE. WEARS GLASSES. THAT'S IT.

MIKE? YOU GOT A POCKET TEST?
YEAH, HOLD ON.

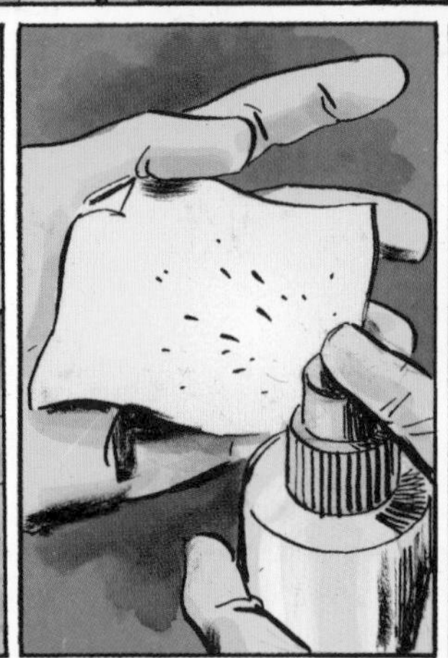

WHAT'D YOU DO WITH IT?
IT'S POSITIVE? FOR WHAT? METH?
WHAT'D YOU DO WITH IT, PARIOS?

HEY, C'MON. *THINK.*
IF I HAD WHATEVER WAS IN THERE, WHY WOULD I *CALL* YOU GUYS? DOES THAT MAKE *SENSE* TO YOU?
CRIMINALS *ARE* NOTORIOUSLY *STUPID.*

WAIT... DID YOU JUST *INSULT* ME?
DEPENDS. ARE YOU A CRIMINAL?
WHAT DID YOU *DO* WITH IT?

I DIDN'T DO ANYTHING WITH "IT"!
THERE WAS NO "IT" TO DO ANYTHING WITH!
NOW, BACK OFF!
SOME "GUY WITH GLASSES" GIVES YOU AN EMPTY GUITAR CASE, TESTS POSITIVE FOR METH RESIDUE?
NAH, IT WASN'T EMPTY.
THERE WAS A GUITAR IN IT, TOO.
YOU THINK WE'RE STUPID?
HIM? NO.
YOU LYING LITTLE--
WHOA, WHOA, WHOA!
EASY THERE, CATHY!
GET OFF ME, MIKE!
YOU THINK I DON'T KNOW HOW THIS PLAYS?
SHE'S GONNA MILK THE ROCK STAR, TURN THIS INTO HER MEAL TICKET.

WRITE A BOOK, MAYBE? SELL THE STORY TO E! OR SOME FUCKING WEBSITE?
WE'RE BRINGING YOU IN FOR **QUESTIONING**.
YEAH, YOU DO THAT, BABY...
...THEN EXPLAIN TO THE D.O.J. WHY THEY'RE SUCKING A METRIC FUCKTON OF LAWSUIT FOR **HARASSMENT** AND **ASSAULT**.
IS THIS **EVIDENCE?** YOU NEED **THIS?**
IT'S EVIDENCE OF A CRIME, YEAH--
THEN FUCKING **TAKE** IT.
IT'S CALLED **RESPECT**.
YOUR PARTNER SHOULD FUCKING **LEARN** SOME.

♪DA DAH
DA DA DA
DAH DAAA♪

PARIOS?
DEX? THIS IS DAVID MAYES. CLICK?

I GOT THAT LIST YOU WANTED, YOU KNOW, OF THE ROADIES?
I WAS THINKING I COULD BRING IT BY YOUR OFFICE?
THAT'D BE *GREAT.*

I'M OUT RIGHT NOW, BUT I SHOULD BE BACK IN ABOUT HALF AN HOUR.
SEE YOU THEN.

--TALK TO ME LIKE THAT AND THEN JUST WALK OUT?!?
WATCH ME, MIM!

AND YOU!
AND ME?
YOU THINK I WASN'T GOING TO FIND OUT?
YOU THINK I WASN'T GOING TO KNOW WHAT YOU TWO HAVE BEEN UP TO?

THAT'S NOT FAIR, TRACY! I TOLD HER NOT TO TELL YOU!
THEN THAT'S THE FIRST TIME SHE'S EVER DONE WHAT SHE'S TOLD!

YOU SHOULD HAVE TOLD ME.
BOTH OF YOU.

YOU SHOULD HAVE TOLD ME.

THAT WAS AWKWARD.
NO KIDDING.

SHE CAME BY, SOMEONE HAD TOLD HER ABOUT THE D.E.A. AND BABY AND YOU AND ALL OF IT.
SHE WANTED TO KNOW WHY I HADN'T COME TO HER, WHY I'D GONE TO YOU INSTEAD.
I'VE BEEN WONDERING THE SAME THING.

SIGH
TRACY AND I WERE TOGETHER FOR SIX MONTHS.

THIS WAS AFTER THE STUFF WITH MY BROTHER, MY FATHER, TAILHOOK...
...THERE'D BEEN SO MUCH MEDIA ATTENTION...
...I JUST WANTED TO GET MY LIFE IN ORDER.

I WANTED TO COME OUT...
...WE HAD THESE FIGHTS...

...SHE SAID...
...SHE DIDN'T WANT TO BE LINDSAY LOHAN'S GIRLFRIEND, YOU KNOW?

COME WITH ME.

I FOUND BABY.

I DIDN'T WANT TO BE DRIVING AROUND WITH IT IN THE MUSTANG.

YOU HAVE ANY IDEA HOW ***MUCH*** THAT GUITAR IS ***WORTH?***

I TOLD YOU BEFORE, STEVEN PAID MAYBE SEVEN FIFTY FOR IT.

I CAN'T TELL IF YOU'RE ***CHARMINGLY NAIVE*** OR JUST PRETENDING.

I DID SOME ***CHECKING.*** WANT TO HEAR HOW MUCH I COULD ***GET*** FOR BABY?

UHM... SURE.

ROUGHLY A QUARTER MILLION.

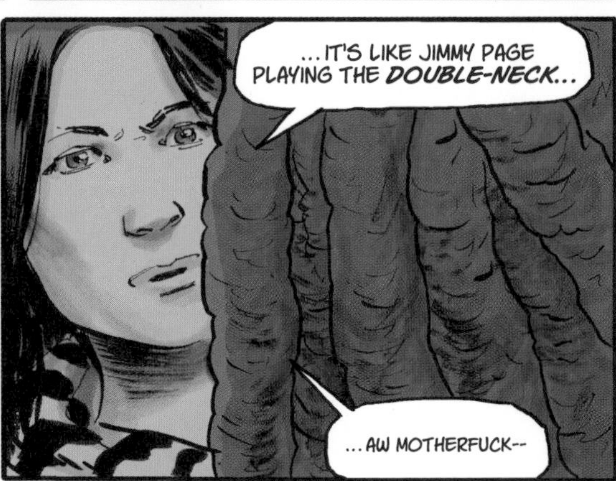

--STAY HERE!
WAIT!
WAIT.
JUST PUT IT DOWN, MAN.
YOU TALKING TO ME?
ARE YOU TALKING TO ME?
MAN, YOUR TRAVIS BICKLE SHIT IS WEAK.
BRAD? IT'S NOT HERE, MAN. THERE'S JUST THE GUITAR!

WHERE IS IT?
WHERE'S WHAT?
UH, BRAD?
SHUT UP, MICK!
WHERE'S OUR STUFF, BOY?
BRAAAD--
GOD DAMMIT, MICK--
--WHAT?!?
HELLO, ASSHOLE.
CLICK? HOW'S BABY?
SAFE AND SOUND.
RIGHT...

...WHICH ONE OF YOU ASSHOLES DO I SHOOT FIRST?

Chapter Four

PEED
IMIT
St John's

OKAY, I CAN SEE THIS GOING A NUMBER OF WAYS.
FIRST, YOU GUYS DO SOMETHING DUMB AND I GET TO SHOOT YOU.
THAT'S HONESTLY MY PREFERENCE. I REALLY DON'T LIKE YOU GUYS.
YOU'RE RACISTS, YOU'RE IDIOTS, YOU'RE VIOLENT, AND YOU BROKE INTO MY OFFICE...
...SO THE SELF-DEFENSE PLEA IS A NO-BRAINER, REALLY.
THE OTHER WAY THIS GOES IS YOU SIT TIGHT WHILE WE WAIT FOR THE COPS OR THE D.E.A. TO ARRIVE.
THEN YOU GET TO TELL THEM ALL ABOUT YOUR LITTLE DRUG-SMUGGLING OPERATION, MAYBE--
BABY!

LET ME SEE HER! IS SHE OKAY?
MIM, DAMMIT, I TOLD YOU TO WAIT OUT--

I'M SORRY! DEX, I'M SO SORRY!
OW OW OW
GRAB HER!

GO, LET'S GO!
GET YOUR HANDS OFF OF ME!

YOU HURT HER, AND I WILL FUCKING SHOOT YOU IN EACH OF YOUR PIGGY LITTLE EYES.
LET HER GO.

I KNOW, I JUST *WANTED* TO--

OW!

WHO?
HER, YOU FUCKING *IDIOT!*

GIVE HER *BACK--*

SHIT!
DAMMIT! *DAMMIT!*

CALL THE POLICE!
MIM--
THEY HAVE BABY!

GO GO GO GO GO!

OH, NOT ON YOUR *LIFE.*

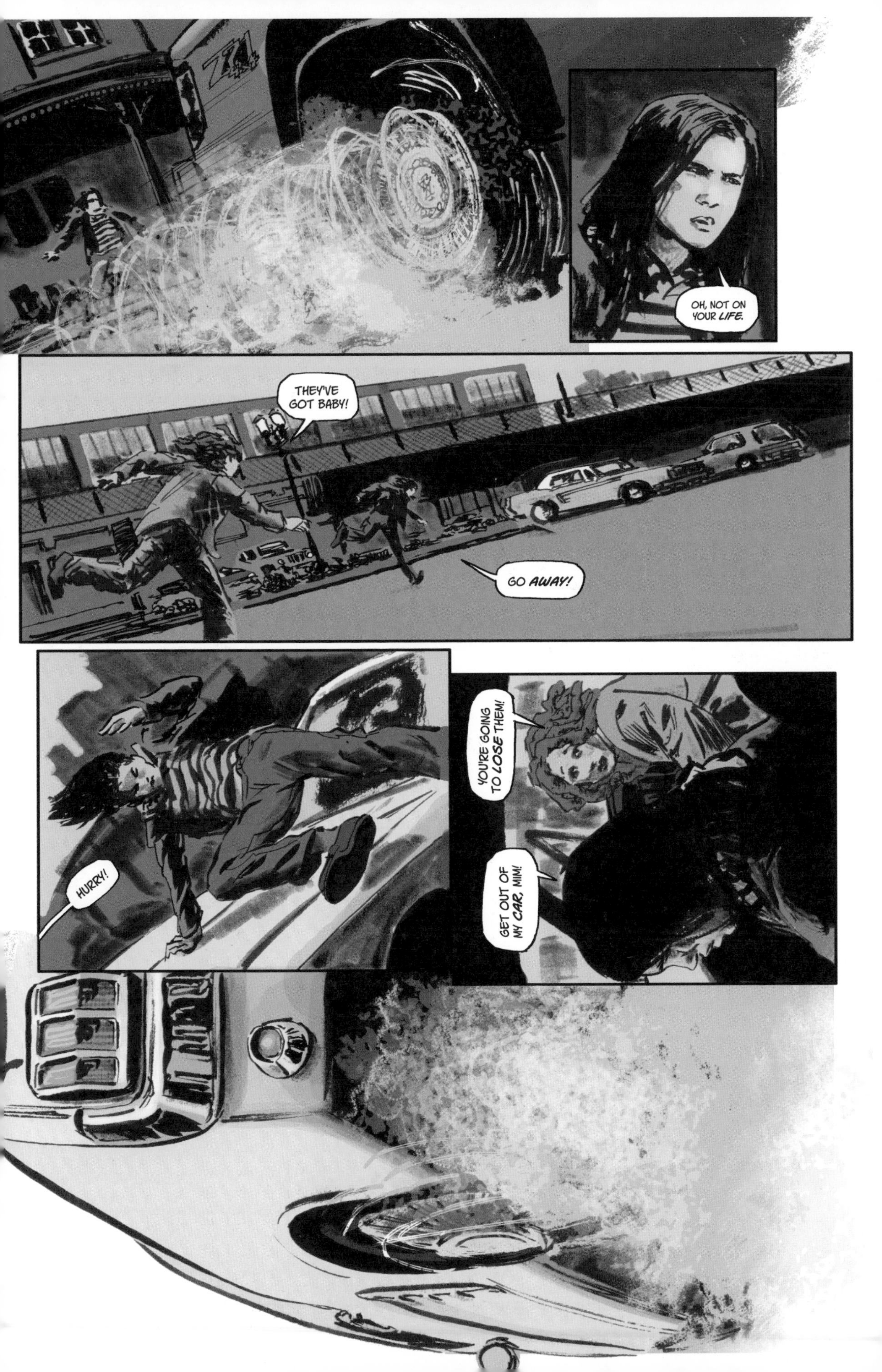

THEY'VE GOT BABY!
GO *AWAY!*

HURRY!
YOU'RE GOING TO *LOSE* THEM!
GET OUT OF MY *CAR,* MIM!

I DON'T SEE THEM!
DON'T *TALK* TO ME!
YOU DON'T *GET* TO TALK TO ME--
--I *TOLD* YOU TO *WAIT*, I *TOLD* YOU TO GET OUT OF MY *CAR*--

DAMMIT, MIM!
PUT ON YOUR *SEATBELT!*
I'M *TRYING!*
YOUR *STUPID* CAR DOESN'T STUPID HAVE ONE!
IT'S A *LAP BELT,* DAMMIT! PUT IT *ON!*
GATX

OH, YOU THINK SO, MOTHERFUCKER?

GET DOWN.
WHAT?
THEY DOING?
GET DOWN!

THEY'RE SHOOTING AT US? WHY ARE THEY SHOOTING AT US?
I THINK MAYBE THEY DON'T WANT US FOLLOWING THEM, MIM.
STAY DOWN.
30

SHIT.
PLEASE DON'T.

ST. JOHN'S BRIDGE...
...I GOT *SHOT* HERE, YOU KNOW THAT?
LET ME *OUT.*
YOU SHOULD'VE *GONE* BEFORE WE LEFT.
I *HAVE* TO GET *OUT* OF THIS *CAR!*
ABOUT FUCKING TIME.
WHAT DOES *THAT* MEAN? IT'S THE *POLICE!*
YOU KNOW WHAT HAPPENS IF I GET *ARRESTED?* WITH *YOU?* LIKE *THIS??*

I'LL BE ON *T.M.Z.* UNTIL THE END OF *TIME!*
MIM--
--SHUT *UP!*
GOTCHA, ASSHOLE...
...YOU JUST RAN OUT OF *ROAD.*

HANDS!

LET ME SEE YOUR ***HANDS!***

NOBODY MOVES.
PORTLAND POLICE
I AM OUT WITH FOUR SUSPECTS SOUTH OF CATHEDRAL PARK AT--
HNHHNN
KRAK
KRAK KRAK KRAK
GET IN THE CAR!

KRAK
MIM!
BABY!
KRAK
ping
YEAH, NO.
MIM! FOR THE LOVE OF GOD--
--RUN!

KRAK
KRAK
KLK
KLK
MICK!
COME ON, DAMMIT!!
PORTLAN
OFFICER DOWN, SHOTS FIRED! THEY TOOK MY UNIT, I REPEAT, TWO SUSPECTS, WHITE MALE--

YOU'RE WILLING TO DIE FOR A GUITAR?
IT'S NOT JUST A GUITAR!
YOU CAN BUY ANOTHER ONE, MIM! YOU CAN BUY FIVE HUNDRED OTHER ONES! YOU'RE RICH!
AW, SHIT!
THAT CAN'T BE THEM.
THAT CAN'T BE THEM!
KEEP SAYING IT, MAYBE THEY'LL BELIEVE YOU.
THEY SHOT A COP, MIM.
THEY DON'T HAVE ANYTHING LEFT TO LOSE.
HOLD ON.

20 30 40 50 60/70 80 90 100
UNIVERSITY OF
20 MPH
UHMM--

--CLIFF CLIFF CLIFF
JESUS CHRIST DEX--
BRAKE
--TURN!!!!
DAMMIT...
...WHERE THE
HELL ARE THE COPS?

60 70 80 90 100 110
ONLY
ONLY

WHAT ARE *WE* DOING? WE'RE JUST *RUNNING* AWAY?
WE'RE GIVING THE *COPS* TIME--
--THEY KNOW THAT *CAR* HAS BEEN STOLEN, ONE OF THEIR OWN HAS BEEN *SHOT*--
--JUST NEED A *ROADBLOCK*...
...OR SOMETHING...
HEH.
YEAH...
HEH? *HEH!?*
...THIS MAY *SUCK*, JUST TO WARN YOU.

WAIT, WHAT ARE YOU *DOING?*
DEX? DEX!
OH MY *GOD.*
OH MY GOD OH MY GOD--
--OHMYGODOHMYGODOHMYGOD--
C'MON.
YOU KNOW YOU *WANT* TO...

KRRNNNCH

SO...
...WAS IT GOOD FOR YOU?

Chapter Five

"--HIGH-SPEED CHASE THROUGH NORTH PORTLAND THAT HAS LEFT ONE OFFICER IN CRITICAL CONDITION...

"...AND RESULTED IN THE CLOSURE OF THE BURNSIDE BRIDGE THIS AFTERNOON FOLLOWING A FOOLHARDY ATTEMPT BY ONE OF THE DRIVERS TO JUMP THE BRIDGE AS IT WAS BEING RAISED...

"...SEEN HERE.
"OF THE VEHICLE'S TWO OCCUPANTS, ONE HAS BEEN IDENTIFIED...
"...MIRIAM BRACCA, MEMBER OF THE PORTLAND-BASED BAND TAILHOOK.

"THE OCCUPANTS OF THE SECOND VEHICLE HAVE NOT BEEN IDENTIFIED...
"...THOUGH SOURCES INDICATE THAT BOTH ARE BEING CHARGED IN CONNECTION WITH THE SHOOTING...

"...AS WELL AS THE THEFT OF A PORTLAND POLICE BUREAU POLICE CAR USED IN THE PURSUIT.

"THE D.E.A. IS SAID TO BE PARTICIPATING IN THE INVESTIGATION...

"...AND WE'LL HAVE MORE ON THIS STORY AS IT DEVELOPS..."
...GIVE IT UP FIRST, YOU OR YOUR CRY-BABY PARTNER?
MY MONEY'S ON YOUR FRIEND, SO IF YOU'RE LOOKING FOR A DEAL, THAT WINDOW IS CLOSING FAST.

...WHO'S THE CONNECTION, EASLEY? GIVE ME A NAME...

INTERVIE
...BELIEVE SHE TRIED TO JUMP THE BRIDGE?
FORGET THAT, YOU SEE WHAT HAPPENED TO HER CAR? FUCKING CRIMINAL...

...DOING THAT TO A VINTAGE MUSTANG...

HEY, TRACY.
ANY WORD ON THE COP THEY *SHOT?*

RENETTO, YEAH. LOOKS LIKE HE'LL BE OKAY.
THANK GOD FOR THAT.

YOU'RE A FUCKING MORON, YOU KNOW THAT, DEX?
WHAT WAS I SUPPOSED TO *DO?* LET THEM GET *AWAY?*
YOU WERE SUPPOSED TO LET THE *COPS* HANDLE THIS!

SO HOW'S THIS GOING TO *PLAY?*
I REALLY DON'T KNOW. I REALLY *DON'T.*

THE D.E.A.'S WORKING YOUR *SKINHEAD* ADMIRERS OVER RIGHT NOW.
THE LITTLE ONE'S BAWLING LIKE A BABY, AND AGENT CHASE IS ABOUT TO HAVE THE OTHER FOR *DINNER.*

AS FOR *MIM*...

...SHE'S GOT SOMETHING LIKE THREE TONS WORTH OF LAWYERS HERE RIGHT NOW TALKING WITH THE ASSISTANT DISTRICT ATTORNEY.
HER MANAGER IS HERE, TOO, AND THE MEDIA'S CAMPED OUT FRONT.

WHICH LEAVES YOU.

ME?

VOLK.

LIEUTENANT VOLK, YES.
HE WANTS TO WEAR MY ENTRAILS FOR A HAT.
MAYBE A NECKLACE.

THEY WERE CHASING US.
NOT AT THE START.
I WAS TRYING TO GET BABY BACK!

BABY?

THE GUITAR! THE GUITAR THAT MIM HIRED ME TO FIND!
I MEAN, WHAT'S VOLK GOING TO CHARGE ME WITH? DOING MY JOB?

HE'S GOT SOMETHING IN THE NEIGHBORHOOD OF THIRTY MOVING VIOLATIONS TO START WITH, I THINK.
JUMPING THE BURNSIDE MIGHT COUNT AS FEDERAL, TOO, I'M NOT SURE.
ARE YOU FUCKING KIDDING ME?
I'LL HAVE TO CHECK. MIGHT BE A HOMELAND SECURITY THING, I DON'T KNOW.

I NEED A LAWYER.
YEAH, I THINK MAYBE YOU--
CUT HER LOOSE.

YOU HEARD ME.
CUT HER LOOSE.

...COURSE BE HAPPY TO ASSIST THE INVESTIGATION IN ANY WAY POSSIBLE. JUST HAVE YOUR PEOPLE CALL MY OFFICE.
YOU'LL WANT TO TAKE THE GARAGE EXIT, WE CAN GET YOU OUT THAT WAY.

AND YOU'LL MAKE A STATEMENT TO THE MEDIA, MAKING IT CLEAR THAT MY CLIENT IS IN NO WAY RESPONSIBLE FOR WHAT TRANSPIRED?
ABSOLUTELY, FRED. NO MEMBER OF THE BAND IS IN ANY WAY INVOLVED IN OUR INVESTIGATION. I'LL STRESS THE POINT.

AND THE D.E.A. AGREES WITH THAT?

I'VE HEARD FROM THEIR OFFICE. THEY'VE NO INTEREST IN YOUR CLIENT.
VERY GOOD.

AND YOU MUST BE PARIOS, YES?
FRED CHAPEL.

YOU'RE MIM'S ATTORNEY, I TAKE IT?
ONE OF THEM. ONE OF THE BAND'S. PLEASURE TO MEET YOU.
LET ME WALK YOU OUT.

WAIT, I'M NOT BEING CHARGED?
CAN'T SEE A NEED AT THIS POINT, PROVIDED YOU'LL MAKE YOURSELF AVAILABLE SHOULD WE NEED YOU.
YOU WERE ACTING AS MISS BRACCA'S AGENT IN THIS AFFAIR...

...WE'VE GOT THE MEN WHO SHOT OUR OFFICER AND WHO WERE CHASING YOU, THAT'S WHERE THE CRIME LIES, AFTER ALL.
UH-HUH.
I'LL BE IN TOUCH, GRANT.

YOU HAVE A PLACE TO STAY? THE PRESS WILL FIND YOU AT YOUR HOME, IT'S PROBABLY BEST TO AVOID THEM.
MISS BRACCA WOULD APPRECIATE YOUR DISCRETION IN ALL THIS...

...THOUGH OF COURSE YOU'RE FREE TO TALK TO WHOEVER YOU WANT, I KNOW SHE'D BE GRATEFUL IF YOU AVOIDED THE MEDIA.
MIGHT BE BEST IF YOU KEPT YOUR HEAD DOWN FOR A FEW DAYS, UNTIL EVERYTHING BLOWS OVER.

BEST FOR YOU, BEST FOR HER. BEST FOR THE BAND.

YOU ASKING ME ON A DATE?

SO THAT'S A NO?
MISS BRACCA THANKS YOU FOR YOUR HELP, MISS PARIOS.
DOES SHE?

SHE HAS HER GUITAR BACK, MISS PARIOS. YOUR JOB WAS TO RETRIEVE IT FOR HER.
FROM WHERE HER MANAGEMENT STANDS, THAT MEANS YOUR INVOLVEMENT WITH HER AND TAILHOOK IS FINISHED.

IT WOULD PROBABLY BE IN EVERYONE'S BEST INTERESTS IF YOU LET THINGS RUN THEIR COURSE FROM HERE ON OUT.
IT'S JUST A SUGGESTION.

I'D EXIT THE BUILDING THROUGH THE GARAGE, IF I WERE YOU.
MORE DISCREET.

NICE MEETING YOU.

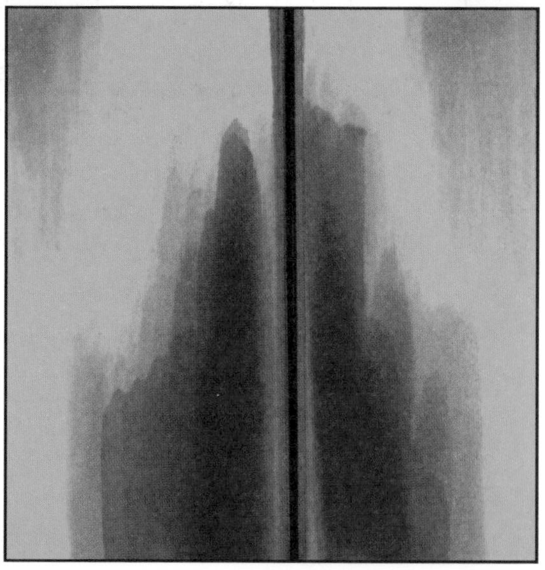

HEY, GREY, IT'S ME--
...OH, YOU SAW THAT, DID YOU? YEAH...

...OH, C'MON, LIKE YOU'VE NEVER WANTED TO TRY IT...
SO, LISTEN, I NEED A FAVOR...YES, ANOTHER ONE. CAN YOU KEEP ANSEL FOR THE NIGHT?
BEEP BEEP

YEAH, THERE'S A CHANCE THE PRESS WILL SHOW UP AT MY PLACE, SO...
NEED A LIFT?
...THANKS, GREY, LISTEN, I'LL CALL YOU BACK.

THANKS, CLICK.
DAVID, REMEMBER?
YOU'VE GOT GOOD TIMING.

ACTUALLY, NO. I WAS WAITING FOR YOU.
REALLY?
NO LIE.

SAW IT ON THE NEWS, HUH?
AH, NO. WELL, YES, BUT I'D CALLED THE COPS FROM YOUR OFFICE AFTER YOU AND MIM BOLTED OUT OF THERE.
SO, WHERE CAN I TAKE YOU?
Jeep

YOU STILL HAVE THAT LIST OF ROADIES?

I DO, YEAH.
WHERE'S MIM?
UHM... HOLED UP AT THE VINTAGE PLAZA, I THINK.
TAKE ME THERE?

THERE'S SOME UNFINISHED BUSINESS...

BUT IT'S OVER.

ISN'T IT OVER? I'VE GOT BABY BACK, THE D.E.A. SAYS I'M NOT A SUSPECT IN ANYTHING.
THEY GOT THE GUYS WHO STOLE THE GUITAR.
ISN'T IT OVER?

HECKEL AND JECKEL DIDN'T STEAL BABY, MIM.
NOT THE FIRST TIME, AT LEAST.

SHE FIGURES IT WAS ONE OF THE ROADIES.
BUT... WHY?
YOU KNOW WHY...

...SOMEONE WAS SMUGGLING DRUGS IN THE BAND'S GEAR.
D.E.A. DID A POCKET TEST ON BABY'S CASE, MIM, IT RANG POSITIVE FOR METH.
MY GUESS IS THAT THEY'D FIND THE SAME RESULT IF THEY TESTED CLICK'S DRUMS OR ANY OF A DOZEN OTHER PIECES OF YOUR ROAD EQUIPMENT.

ONE OF THE ROADIES.

NOT JUST ONE OF THE ROADIES.
SOMEONE GAVE BABY BACK. SOMEONE GAVE BABY BACK TO ME.
WHICH MEANS WHOEVER THAT WAS, HE OR SHE KNEW I WAS WORKING FOR YOU.

WHO?
AH, AND HERE WE COME TO THE QUESTION, MY DEAR.
WHO IN THE ROAD CREW WOULD STEAL YOUR GUITAR ONLY TO MAKE SURE IT GOT BACK TO YOU?

I DON'T... I MEAN, I CAN'T...
WHY WOULD SOMEONE DO THAT?

SAME REASON I CAME TO SEE DEX, HERE.
THAT'S WHAT YOU'RE SAYING, ISN'T IT, DEX?
THAT'S WHAT I'M SAYING, DAVID.

I DON'T KNOW WHY CLICK WENT TO YOU.
I DIDN'T EVEN KNOW THAT CLICK WENT TO YOU.

MIMSER, RELAX. I WENT TO DEX BECAUSE I WAS WORRIED ABOUT YOU.
THAT'S WHAT SHE'S SAYING...

...WHOEVER TOOK BABY, IT WAS SOMEONE TRYING TO LOOK OUT FOR YOU.
CAN YOU THINK OF ANYONE LIKE THAT FROM THE TOUR? ANYONE WHO MADE IT A POINT TO LOOK AFTER YOU?

FABRIZIO... BUT YOU TALKED TO HIM...
...I CAN'T... I MEAN, I NEVER ASKED FOR ANYTHING, I'M NOT VAN OR...

SOMEONE WHO WORE GLASSES. A GUY WHO WORE GLASSES.

...OH! OH, WAIT...
DANNY!

DANNY PERKINS! HE WOULD HAVE ICE FOR ME BETWEEN SETS, AND HE ALWAYS MADE SURE I HAD WATER, EXTRA WATER.
AND PICKS! HE ALWAYS HAD PICKS FOR ME!
AND HE WEARS GLASSES!

DAVID?
CHECKING...

...GOT HIM...
...AND HE LIVES HERE IN TOWN...
DANIEL PERKINS

NOK NOK NOK NOK NOK

I SAID I WAS ***COMING,*** JESUS ***CHRIST,*** MAN...

TAILHOOK

THE BLACK KEYS

HARVEY DANGER

—the last time I let you hold meee—

SHOULD BE APARTMENT SEVEN...
HEY.
--sang it to me so sweetly--

YOU?
THAT'S *US.*
THE *MUSIC,* I MEAN.
words like honey in my ear--

--Claudius pouring your poison in my ear--
GUY'S ***OLD SCHOOL!*** DIGS HIS ***VINYL.***
"TERMINAL LIES," CLICK! LISTEN! YOU REMEMBER?

I REMEMBER VAN THROWING A ***HISSY*** OVER BEING ***AUTO-TUNED.***
STILL PLAYING...
and your words, only words, corrupting words and ohhh--

...CAN'T HAVE BEEN ***LONG,*** THEN...
--say it again, say it again, I'm dying for more--

...CALL ***TRACY!***
--more of your terminal lies--

CAN'T HAVE GONE FAR,
CAN'T HAVE GONE FAR...

...UNLESS THEY LEFT IN A **CAR** IN WHICH CASE THEY **HAVE** GONE **FAR** AND I'M TOTALLY **FUCKED...**

...WHICH WOULD BE **PAR** FOR THE **COURSE,** REALLY, WAY THINGS HAVE BEEN **GOING...**

...WAY THINGS HAVE BEEN...
...GOING...
14 88

KOF KOFF I D-DON'T--
I HOPE YOU'RE LYING, KID, I REALLY DO.

THERE WERE FIVE POUNDS OF CRYSTAL IN THAT CASE.
THAT'S FIVE POUNDS BELONGING TO ME THAT YOU STOLE.
YOU KNOW HOW MUCH FIVE POUNDS OF CRYSTAL IS WORTH?

ALMOST HALF A MILLION DOLLARS, THAT'S HOW MUCH.
SO I'M ASKING YOU AGAIN...

...WHERE'S MY CRYSTAL, BOY?

D-DON'T UNDERSTAND I D-DIDN'T... DIDN'T MEAN TO...
...FOUND IT BY ACCIDENT...
...DIDN'T WANT ANYTHING ...ANYTHING TO HAPPEN TO THE BAND...

...WAS TRYING TO PROTECT THE B-BAND...

WHERE'S MY CRYSTAL!
YOU FUCKING LIMP-DICK MOTHERFUCKER, WHERE'S MY STUFF?!?

YOU
HE GAVE IT TO ME.

I HAVE IT.
5150

LET HIM GO AND I'LL TAKE YOU TO IT.

YOU'LL TAKE ME TO IT? YOU WILL?

AND WHO THE FUCK ARE YOU?

NO, I DON'T CARE. YOU KNOW WHAT? I DON'T FUCKING CARE.
AND NO, I WILL NOT LET HIM GO AND YES, YOU WILL TELL ME WHERE IT IS RIGHT NOW...

...OR I WILL MAKE YOU TELL ME, YES, I WILL DO THAT, LITTLE BITCH.

SHIT.
OKAY, ALL RIGHT, I'LL TAKE YOU TO IT...

YOU KNOW WHAT I DO IF YOU'RE LYING TO ME?
GOT A PRETTY GOOD IDEA, YEAH.

THAT'S IT, IT'S IN THE JEEP.

GET IT.

GO ON, GET IT.
NOW, THAT IS A BIG FUCKING GUN...

D.E.A.

JAMES LLWELLYN, YOU'RE UNDER *ARREST.*

DROP THE GUN, ASSHOLE.

YOU TOLD HIM IT WAS IN MY JEEP?
I KNEW YOU GUYS HAD CALLED TRACY. SEEMED THE BEST BET.
226PES

BETTER THAN SHOOTING IT OUT WITH THEM, I GUESS.
ANYTHING IS BETTER THAN SHOOTING IT OUT, CLICK.
BELIEVE ME.
WHAT'RE THEY DOING WITH DANNY?

THEY'RE ARRESTING HIM.
BUT HE GAVE BABY BACK!
HEY, MORON.

I ASSUME YOU MEAN ME, AGENT CHASE?
YES, YOU. THAT WAS FUCKING STUPID OF YOU.
BUT IT WORKED OUT.

WHAT'D HE DO WITH THE METH?
CLAIMS HE THREW IT IN THE WILLAMETTE. I EXPECT HE'S TELLING THE TRUTH. WON'T TAKE LONG TO VERIFY.
KID PANICKED WHEN HE FOUND IT...

...SAYS HE DIDN'T EVEN KNOW ABOUT THE SMUGGLING UNTIL HE WAS STORING THE GUITAR BACK IN ITS CASE, SAW THAT THE LINING WAS TORN UP.

HE THOUGHT IT WAS HERS.
DEX WAS RIGHT? HE WAS TRYING TO PROTECT ME?
NOT YOU. HE WAS TRYING TO PROTECT THE BAND...

...IT WAS ALL ABOUT THE MUSIC, HE SAYS.

I GET THAT THE SKINHEADS WERE THE CONNECTION ON THIS END.
WHAT I'M WONDERING IS WHO PUT IT THERE IN THE FIRST PLACE.
YOU AND ME BOTH. BUT WE'VE GOT LLWELLYN IN CUSTODY...

...WE'LL KNOW THE ANSWER SOON ENOUGH...

MITCH.
MITCH.
MITCH.
GO BY TRAIN
UNION STATION

I KNOW SHE'S TOTALED, I'M ASKING YOU HOW MUCH IT'LL COST TO FIX HER.

...THAT MUCH?
...NO...

...I'LL HAVE TO GET BACK TO YOU...

HEY.

MIM! HEY! I THOUGHT YOU WERE STILL IN HIDING FROM THE PRESS.
HOW'RE YOU?
GOOD, I'M GOOD.

COME WITH ME, I'VE GOT SOMETHING TO SHOW YOU.

MIM--
JUST FOLLOW ME, OKAY?

SO YOU GOT THE **CHECK** FOR YOUR **BILL,** I KNOW, BUT CLICK AND I WERE **TALKING** ABOUT EVERYTHING YOU DID...
NO. YOU'RE KIDDING ME. NO.

...AND WE DECIDED YOU DESERVE A **BONUS.**

I...
...I...
...I...

...I...
...UH...

...A *BETTER* PERSON WOULD *REFUSE.*
I AM *NOT* THAT BETTER PERSON.

GOOD.
HERE. YOU *TWO* SHOULD GET TO *KNOW* EACH OTHER.

SEE YOU AROUND, GUMSHOE.

KRRNCH

OH, GOD! OH, GOD, WOW, I'M *SORRY*...

...I THOUGHT I HAD THE *TURN*, I'M SORRY...

...YOU CAN GET THAT *REPAIRED*, RIGHT? YOU CAN GET THAT *REPAIRED*...

"...IT'S ONLY MONEY, RIGHT?"
MR. MARENCO?

TELL ME.
WE LOST THE SHIPMENT. HALF A MILLION DOLLARS WORTH.
D.E.A. HAS LLWELLYN IN CUSTODY.

CAN HE HURT US?
NO, SIR.

SEE WHAT CAN BE DONE ABOUT A REPLACEMENT.
ALREADY WORKING ON.
GOOD.
WILLIAM?
YES, MISTER MARENCO?

FIND OUT WHAT WENT WRONG.
THEN MAKE SURE IT NEVER HAPPENS AGAIN.
YES, SIR.

Artist Bios

GREG RUCKA was born in San Francisco and raised on the Central Coast of California, in what is commonly referred to as "Steinbeck Country." He began his writing career in earnest at the age of 10 by winning a county-wide short-story contest, and hasn't let up since. He graduated from Vassar College with an A.B. in English, and from the University of Southern California's Master of Professional Writing program with an M.F.A.

He is the author of nearly a dozen novels, six featuring bodyguard Atticus Kodiak, and three featuring Tara Chace, the protagonist of his *Queen & Country* series. Additionally, he has penned several short-stories, countless comics, and the occasional non-fiction essay. In comics, he has had the opportunity to write stories featuring some of the world's best-known characters—Superman, Batman, and Wonder Woman—as well as penning several creator-owned properties himself, such as *Whiteout* and *Queen & Country*, both published by Oni Press. His work has been optioned several times over, and his services are in high-demand in a variety of creative fields as a story-doctor and creative consultant.

Greg resides in Portland, Oregon, with his wife, author Jennifer Van Meter, and his two children. He thinks the biggest problem with the world is that people aren't paying enough attention.

MATTHEW SOUTHWORTH is a musician, playwright, filmmaker, and cartoonist who has lived in Nashville, Los Angeles, Louisville, Pittsburgh, and now Seattle.

He used to lead a band called the Capillaries, and they never broke up. He directed an independent feature film that he very nearly finished. He came this close to getting his Masters in playwriting and directing from Carnegie Mellon University.

He has undiagnosed (but undeniable) attention deficit disorder and has trouble sitting still long enough to get his work done. Nonetheless, in addition to *Stumptown*, he has drawn comics for Marvel, DC, and Image.

RICO RENZI is an artist and designer from Washington D.C.. His work has appeared in WIRED and Fast Company Magazines, and various publications from D.C., Marvel, Image, Dark Horse, Scholastic, Boom Studios, Oni Press and IDW. He currently colors *Spider-Gwen* and *Unbeatable Squirrel Girl* every month and resides in Charlotte, North Carolina with his